First published in 2014 by
The Dedalus Press
13 Moyclare Road
Baldoyle
Dublin 13
Ireland

www.**dedaluspress**.com

Copyright © Theo Dorgan

ISBN 978 1 906614 98 0

Dedalus Press titles are represented in the UK by
Central Books, 99 Wallis Road, London E9 5LN
and in North America by Syracuse University Press, Inc.,
621 Skytop Road, Suite 110, Syracuse, New York 13244.

Printed in Dublin by Gemini International Ltd.

Cover design: Pat Boran

The Dedalus Press receives financial assistance from
The Arts Council / An Chomhairle Ealaíon

NINE BRIGHT SHINERS

Theo Dorgan

DEDALUS PRESS
DUBLIN, IRELAND

ACKNOWLEDGEMENTS

Acknowledgements are due to the editors of the following periodicals or papers where some of these poems, or versions of them, first appeared:

The Irish Times, The Guardian, The SHOp, The Yellow Nib, Poetry Salzburg, Southword, Prairie Schooner (USA), Poetry Ireland Review, Cork Literary Review, The Chaffin Review (USA) and The Penny Dreadful.

Thanks are also due to the editors and publishers of the following books or anthologies:

Voices at the World's Edge (ed. Paddy Bushe), Shine On (ed. Pat Boran), The Golden Bough (Dublin City Galleries), John Shinnors (Wexford Arts Centre), Watching My Hands at Work (Eds. Eva Bourke, Megan Buckley & Louis De Paor), The European Constitution in Verse (eds. David Van Reybrouck, Peter Vermeersch), A Fine Statement (ed. John McDonagh) If Ever You Go (eds. Pat Boran, Gerard Smyth), The Poetry of Men's Lives (eds. Fred Moramarco, Al Zolynas), The Clifden Anthology (ed. Brendan Flynn), Wasting Time With People (ed. Alice Leahy), Best of Irish Poetry 2009 (eds. Paul Perry, Nuala Ní Chonchúir) Honouring The Word (ed. Barbara Brown), Songs of Earth and Light (Southword Editions), Dogs Singing (ed. Jessie Lendennie), Days Like These (with Tony Curtis, Paula Meehan; ed. Samuel Green) and The Lighter Craft (eds. Kevin Honan, Chris Morash).

'Crossing The Border' was set to music by Howard Goodall and is available as CD and score from Faber Music on Winter Lullabies.

Poems in this collection have been broadcast on RTÉ Radio 1, BBC Radio 4, TG4, NPR and RF1.

Contents

✧

ॐ

CHORUS

ॐ

THE SEA, THE SEA

❧

HOUSE OF ECHOES

❧

For my brothers and sisters
with love

I'll sing you twelve, O!
Green grow the rushes, O!
What are your twelve, O?
Twelve for the twelve Apostles
Eleven for the eleven who went to heaven,
Ten for the ten commandments,
Nine for the nine bright shiners,
Eight for the April Rainers,
Seven for the seven stars in the sky,
Six for the six proud walkers,
Five for the symbols at your door,
Four for the Gospel makers,
Three, three, the rivals,
Two, two, the lily-white boys,
Clothèd all in green O!
One is one and all alone
And evermore shall be so.

'Green Grow the Rushes O!'
Traditional folk song

Messages from the World

The Angel of History

In the Parliament house on Kildare Street the lamps were
    burning.
It was a winter night, the usual slant rain falling.

I had paused to light up a cigarette, to watch the lone Guard
stamp her feet, blow uselessly into her cupped, gloved hands.

In the colonnade of the National Library a man was standing,
a man neither old nor young, his head bare, half turned towards

the lights in the Parliament house, the high blank windows.
I saw him reach inside his long loose coat, take out a notebook.

I crossed the road, gathering my own long coat around me,
stood in behind him, looked over his shoulder. He paid no
    heed.

One after another I saw him strike them out from a long list
    of names:
Senators, Deputies, Ministers. One after another the names

dissolved on the page, a scant dozen remaining. I watched him
ink in a question mark after each of these, neat and precise.

He put the book away, sliding it down carefully into a deep
    pocket;
he turned and looked at me, nothing like pity in those hollow
    eyes.

He sighed, then squared his shoulders, lifted his face to the rain
and was gone. Gone as if he had never been. But I saw him,

I know who he was, I witnessed that cold, exact cancellation;
walked on, walked home, thoughtful, afraid for my country.

All Time is Not the Same Time

She wasn't begging, not exactly.
Just sitting out of the flow.

She wasn't sitting, not exactly.
She was just there, out of the flow.

I wasn't hurrying, not exactly.
Just walking, going with the flow.

Well, not just walking,
I was worrying my way through the flow.

She looked up, and smiled.
Just that, she smiled

and I smiled back.
Of course I did.

I reached in my pocket
but she shook her head,

she held my eyes
and let her look fall,

out of the hurting world,
out of the flow.

Time on the River

1.

We push upriver against the fading day,
the current broad and strong,
our boat low in the water.
I stand on the afterdeck, tumbled about
by great vaults of light; bright clouds
high in the west. We plough on
steady and sure, the diesel's reliable hum
beneath my feet, the polished ash
of the tiller warm in my grip.
All day we have been out of time, silent
and comfortable with it, borne up
on the brown, turbid river,
making north steadily towards evening
and a berth at Clonmacnoise.

Time on the river is deep and slow,
you said so this morning, coming up
with tea for the helm.
You were stood at my shoulder,
gazing back down the beaded wake,
a small shiver in your neck,
your cropped head warm on my ear.
Deep and slow, you said again,
and I felt it opening in my bones.
The weight of the river fell against us
on a long, dark curve and we leaned,
hip to hip, to bring the bow around,
at one with the boat, the river and each other,
subtracted from the known world.

2.

The sun sank in the callows to the west.
We heard curlews, that high lonesomeness;
mallards creaked by, four swans
broke down the air and battered past.
You'd flaked out a mooring line on deck,
I was eyeing up the jetties dead ahead ...

A wall of cold air crashed through us,
the long clatter of oars, a mounting roar
and something swept through from behind,
doubling our boat, then on out ahead —
dragon prow, bloodlust, rank fetid blast.
The church roof blazed; towers shook, then steadied.
Time shock. The fall of evening. Clonmacnoise.

Crossing the Border

Bells break on the winter air,
the trees are cased in ice.
The wind blows
through blinding snow
and day is near.

Blue on the winter air,
the flaring border lights.
The wind blows
through driving snow
and help is near.

The road from the frontier post goes
beside a lake that's frozen hard.
They make us stand here in the cold
and look upon the promised land.

Ní fada uainn anois an lá
Má mhairimid, má fhanann beo

Home is where they broke our hearts
and burned our houses, laid us low;
beyond the lake that's frozen hard
the city where we hope to go.

Harsh song on the winter air,
somebody's crying child.
The wind blows
through blinding snow
and freezes tears.

Bells break on the winter air,
the trees are cased in ice.
The wind blows
through blinding snow
and day is near.

Ní fada uainn anois an lá
Má mhairimid, má fhanann beo

Police Check

In order to frighten us, he reads out a list of names:
Victor Jara, Salvador Allende ...
In order to sober him, we recite a list of names:
Salvador Allende, Victor Jara ...

Family Tree

Under the bone-white moon of Granada I name you,
Federico García Lorca, who lived and died for love.
Under the golden mosaic of Ravenna I name you,
Dante Alighieri, hopelessly importuning your Beatrice.

Nadezhda Mandelstam I name, who hoped against hope
and then abandoned hope but never her undying love.
In the darkest of nights these flames will keep on burning,
no storm, no steel, no cold can quench these flames.

One after another I light my candles to human love,
to all those in the wind, blown through the world like leaves,
to those gone to the bonfires, the furnace of history,
to all those who struggled for bread a moment in this life.

It Goes On

It goes on, Federico, it goes on —
in the hearts of the functionaries
who despise the poor they serve,
in the boots of the black-robed priest
who would crucify Christ for impertinence,
in the shop steward breaking the strikers,
the butcher with his dreams of Franco,
the journalist with his special pleading for power,
the investment specialist blank in his lust for gold.

The black horses clip sparks from the stone
in the alleys and shaded laneways of the city,
and the poor tense in their sleep as the patrol goes by —
the children in doorways in Santiago,
the hookers in doorways in Washington DC,
the methadone runaways in Dublin,
women all over the world as the bars shut —
they tense in their sleep, holding themselves close.
And always the cars at night, marked and unmarked.

It goes on, Federico, it goes on —
and still the bone moon rises
on lovers walking the lonesome road home,
cascando somewhere from a darkened room,
a dog crossing between streetlights,
somebody whistling him to the open door;
this, too, goes on and soon it will be morning
where the river sweeps everything into the sea.

Stopping to Catch My Breath, I Heard a Voice

The snow came sweeping down through the dark wood,
the tree-tops clear above the driving snow,
I climbed to where the house of night still stood,
the path my mother climbed so long ago.

The path my father made so long ago,
the house he built where once a broad oak stood,
the tree that fell beneath a weight of snow
and gave him these great beams of time-dark wood.

Their voices echo down the deep of time,
sweep past me through the wood and down the hill.
How many souls have made this heavy climb,
how many are they who must make it still?

How many are there who must make it still,
put down their burdens, face into this climb
that leads to the bright stars above the hill,
the vault of heaven overarching time?

The vault of heaven stands above the roof.
I light a fire inside, throw wide the door,
I let the blaze shine out as living proof
my people keep their bargain with the poor.

My people keep their bargain with the poor,
this fire at heart of winter living proof:
Once we were made the keepers of the door,
all are made welcome under this wide roof.

after Jean Berger's 'Les tuteurs de l'infini'

23

The Buddha in Connemara

I stood in Clifden, watching the tide come in,
thinking about the teacher Brendan Flynn.
Dust hung on the wind, I watched it sway
in a glinting curtain out across the bay.

These particles of dust are not particles of dust,
that is why they are truly particles of dust.

Back in the town the lights were coming on,
and everywhere there was music, dancing, song.

There are in that Buddha country swans, curlews and peacocks.
Three times every night, and three times every day,
they come together and perform a concert,
each uttering his own note.
And from them thus uttering proceeds a sound
proclaiming the five virtues, the five powers,
and the seven steps leading towards the highest knowledge.

I turned and strolled to where a mountain ash
hung its bright beads across the brown stream's dash
down from the heathery heights and the cold blow
headlong into the sea below.

Within a clear, cool cloud, there should not be
a sudden blazing clash of thunder.

How much we learn from those who are truly good,
the thought struck me unbidden where I stood.

All of you should have an upright mind,
and take a straightforward disposition as your basis.

I stand in Clifden, watching the tide come in,
thinking about that wise man, Brendan Flynn.

The Lost Gaeltacht of Lower Manhattan

The yellow cabs tick downtown in the rain,
sparked electrons in the bright-lit veins.

Siúl a rún ó. Ná siúl. Siúl.

Like grace notes the elevators rise and fall,
staff notation on the sheet-glass walls.

Fuaim ag an macalla. Mo chúl le balla.

On the ferry to Station Island the turnstile clicks.
Silence, a brooding absence above the Styx.

Ar bhruach linne 'sea do lonnaigh mo chlann.

Badged, whitehaired, the ticket-collector comes around.
'Murphy', I read — 'Murchú", I say, sea hound.

"Cad as duit féin?" fiafraíonn sé. "Corcaigh?

There's nothing but money here, I'd sooner go home."
But I know he won't, he sees it in my eyes.

Tóraíocht, deoraíocht, toradh luí beirte.

We turn to the Statue, her torch of empty air.
"Tell me," he asks, "do they still speak Irish over there?"

for Peter Sirr

Three Heterodox Sonnets
for John Shinnors

1.

Stone, water, colour, air —
fog of being,
getting there.

Grey, blue, heavy, thin
wash of water
out and in.

You fly like a kite in air,
you swim like a fish in sea.
You sit like a stone in a wall, you stand
like sticks and stone on the land.

Nothing is ever lost
and nothing is ever gained, except
you stand for as long as you can, silent —
you summon the will to paint.

2.

The fields in February are black and white,
colour subtracted from the liquid air.
You know this when you learn to see it right,
the hedgebone architecture stiff and bare.

The estuary water is cold silk,
day draws a breath of frost, a witch's kiss.
The white of dawn is not the white of milk —
you reach a hand to touch, you fear you'll miss.

The world you see is all that is the case,
the world you make is now the world that is,
you hover in twin airs above the race;
in two minds you ask yourself: riddle me this.

Ned Kelly's iron mask is in the pond,
you see this when you look. You look beyond.

3.

The river curves out beyond Kilkee, luminous and terrible the
weight of it, the sweep of it.

We are such small beings in the scale of things, a body now in
the current would be a fly in the updraft, a twig in the
turning flood.

Mountainous masses of grey luminous air are tumbled
broadside over the land, the weight enormous on the
sodden fields.

It is the very stuff of nightmare, the unbearable solitude of
feeling all this, being powerless to resist yet having to go on.

Out of the dark one day beyond Kilkee a sudden flash of yellow
light, a kite dancing, a tiny hero grounding in grey rain.

Out in the murk where air and water, salt and spume and spray
made one thick atmosphere a stone tower flashed. And
flashed again.

Rain was driving in slant curtains against the sea, falling in slant
weighted drapes against the land

and on a bare headland, heedless, beyond brave, a scarecrow
held out his shield and sword against the grave.

Out on Loop Head the Famine ghosts have the eyes of Michael
Hartnett, hurt and strange;

when we walk on this earth we do well to remember no place is
unpeopled, it is all *temenos*, sacred ground.

What should we do except paint, talk, sing and be damned? We
   are strangers here and at home where we are most lonely,

most lonely where we are most at home. Much of our world has
   fallen into the sea and the stone half-circle on the
   promontory

has done with fuss, has nothing, wants nothing to do with us. A
   man with a kite snagged in his head might paint all this

if he knew his trade, if he had the touch, if all gone before him
   would show him the way.

A Child Paints Christmas

Against midwinter dark she sets a light
in a gable window;
stark on a wall of black, a dab of white.

The rain falls on a yellow field of frost,
through the lights of Christmas
on the desperate and the lost.

The World as Exhibition

It's after midnight.
In the old blue house
the lovers sit quiet;
silence comes over
the snow-field outside
where it's day and night —
day for the proud child
in the red jumper,
night for the new king
in his yellow crown.
It is night on the lake,
day on the spreading inlet.

Under a blue moon
someone is hanging
our green lovely earth
in a quiet sky.
It is neither day
nor night. Time is away.

The hand is dealt now,
you are free to choose.
The book is a gift
you can choose to read,
the red barn's a gift
you can choose to own.
Everything is free,
everything is now.

It's after midnight
in the bathing-pool,

the air is tender,
someone is humming
a requiem for
an old country lane.
What was lost is found.
The angel's bright shield
is in the orchard,
there are red roses
between you and the
view to the city.

J.J. Cale sings blues
under a blue moon:
"After midnight, we're
gonna let it all hang out."
Time is now,
time is always now.

You can cut the cards,
you can pick the flowers,
you can pick the tunes,
you can say this field
of yellow-gold corn
is a circus tent,
you can break your heart
for the lonesome child
in the bright red cloak,
you can bless the child
in its mother's arms —
you get to decide,
you bring what you need;
everything is free,
everything is now.
Gauds, lines and colours,
paint and raw canvas,

tricks and sleights of hand,
cards of a gambler,
fierceness of the heart,
things half-remembered
that you never knew —
this is what we do:
we take the world you know,
we make it new.

'Lifeboat': Artist Unknown

A wave comes tumbling from electric air,
the maelstrom dark is hurling and pounding you
round, you fear you'll ground on a lee shore
or be battered down soundless forever into the
swallowing fathomless absence of earth's light.

You rally the crew by will and heart, by craft
and order, the body's power of command —
somewhere ashore they are leaping from their beds,
a calm voice on the radio is your lifeline to that harbour
where powerful engines are turning over, lines
are being slipped and the spray lashing your face here
is sweeping the deck of the lifeboat turning out for you.

You hold on, you keep it steady, you watch for the orange flash
in the thundering climbing sea that signals
you are not abandoned, you are not cast out,
a boat is coming to lift you home.
Voices are calling as you pitch and roll,
a net of voices reaching towards you:
dear friend we do not know, they say,
hold on, stand fast, we are coming to bring you home.

i.m. Charlie Hennessy

A Woman in Winter

She walks the ditch, contented and alone,
sends up a flight of crows with every stone.

Beyond the ridge, beyond the frost-gripped fence
the light pours down on lands of innocence.

A tree stands out against the winter snow,
a tree her mother planted years ago.

The sun flares up, and shines through bitter cold
on sudden flashing ornaments of gold.

Aftermath

1.

Outside a cave in the high dry mountains
a man squats on his heels, his eye drawn
to a hawk circling high in the blue of night.

Taking a deep, cold breath he makes the call.

Half a world away, a thin young man shaves
in cold water, pats his face dry, accepts the telephone
and listens. Nothing now left to say.

Midway between these sparking points,
as the arc leaps from mouth to ear,
another man startles in his bed.

The stars look down, unwinking. He subsides.

2.

She gathers briefcase, phone and keys,
looks once around her, tugs at her jacket hem —
dawn light in the hallway crisp and clear.

A look of her mother in the mirror,
something of her father in those eyes.
A life so far away. She turns to go,

then scratches on a yellow pad "Tonight. Phone home."

Hours earlier in Dublin a man stood in his garden,
drinking down lungfuls of September air, struck
by a vision of children on the leaf-bracked lawn.

3.

How slow planes look when heavy banked on air,
you feel the weight of them in the thunder of engines,
a sense of the fore-ordained in the long, slow inward curve —

did she glance out and see it hanging there,
set level towards her? Did she know what was coming?
Did she reach for her bag, somebody's hand, the phone?

What was he thinking of, clean-shaved, there in the cockpit,
the glass wall accelerating towards him,
a window opening into a mountain cave?

How can we know? We'll never know.

4.

House to back wall, house to back wall, clean
and methodical he cuts and cuts, the engine
ticking out across the suburb, steady and sure.

And the phone rings.

He switches off, looks back over his shoulder.
A crow crawks out into the clear blue,
he walks towards the echoing, dark house,

he disappears from view.

5.

Autumn turned over into winter; the garden
lay silent, nothing flew above the half-cut lawn,
a broad stripe pared to the bone,

a swathe of lank grasses, seed heads bowed.

The house was a well of grief. Silence
poured out of it and kept on pouring
into the garden, over the wall,

out over the houses, into our dumbstruck lives.

A call plunged from a satellite and a family died,
the pieces falling forever, blast shards
from the mirror of shadows, unbearable rain.

The same rain falling all over the world.

6.

He cut the lawn at last. We watched him do it.
House to back wall. House to back wall.
Crows called to the engine. Stutter. Cacophony.

Step by step, house to back wall, he laid it all bare.

He never looked up, but he knew we were there,
willing him on, unable to speak or move.
The light died and he stood there under the silence,

and we stood there with him until it was full dark,

in our own pockets of shock, in our own stricken mortality
shook and unsure, alone with our thoughts.
The stars came out and hung in the high cold air.

House by house, light by light, we spoke back across the void.

The Dead Stand All Around Us

Travelling Soul Sutra for Dave Caffrey

The wind is in from the Atlantic.
Oh do not close the window,
let the night beat salt into the room,
let the travelling soul find rest.

The wind is in from the south-west,
from a small graveyard at the sea's edge
where our friend lies with the long grass
under a faint haze of stars.

I hear the sea's long thunder across the bar,
I hear the rain come sweeping down the hill,
his voice at the window like a dipping tern
calling at night from far out at sea.

Oh hold the window open, love, for me
when the time comes, when the wind comes.
Let the night beat salt into the room,
let the travelling soul find rest.

The wind is in from the south-west,
and Dave is lying under gravel, earth and roots
who was a friend to learning and a good man.
His bones are settled now, his soul is travelling on.

Wild Orchids, Windflowers

The long lane curves out beside the lake,
swagged mist in the hawthorns either side.
Leaf rot in the ditches, dust on the verge,
green tunnel of ash and silver birch.

Time you were taking your way to the land of the dead.

The lane joins a country road, drops to the valley.
Bridge then, stone arch, birds in the stream.
Out into sun, a broad land of fields; the long hill
upward, light breaking everywhere on rock,

Time thick in your throat on the road to the land of the dead.

Now the wide highway, built in these last years.
Turn to the west, walk on into the shadow
of your self, this self you made in the long afternoons —
the pen laid down, hand flat on the board.

Evening now, still quiet, on the road to the land of the dead.

Then finally, there up ahead, the wall of stars.
The black vault of time, the heft of glory — you turn,
you fall back along your march,
down the broad highway, the road, the funneling lane,

back the long journey from the land of the quiet dead

to the house under the trees. Light in the window, voices;
lamp on the deal table, a glass of whiskey, a pen.

Blackbird rustling under the laurel, woodsmoke;
you settle your shoulders, you lift the latch, you step in.

i.m. John McGahern, 1934–2006

A Light was Burning

high over Merrion Square
and I crossed to the railings to look up
before I remembered. The shock
was the simplest thing you could feel,
a sense of nothing under your feet.

We walk in such peril of small things.
A light burning late over the Square,
sign of a life that is no more, and then
that vertigo of the dark, silence
more eloquent than a Charlie Parker solo.

Nobody up there rapt in a book of Mahon's,
or the intricate filigree of John McLaughlin;
nobody staring blue-eyed into space
thinking how far we have come,
how far we have to go.

I walked on. It was late, and I was late
and that part of our lives is over.
Now a light burning signals not presence but
absence, our friend who will not come again.
The whole map is shifted that was plain.

i.m. Lar Cassidy 1950–1997

The Laughing Girl

Midsummer, the road opening down into the valley,
the laughing girl on the road, walking away from us
and down there in the trees, by the bridge over the river,
her brothers and father and sisters and her mother, smiling —

out of our arms and into theirs, the laughing girl on the road.
And the ash was late this year but the leaves are out at last,
and up above Thomas Davis Street the pipe band is rehearsing,
the old and the new interweaving, the thread unbroken.

Play me the old tunes, I tell the recording angel, the ones she
    loved,
the ones she danced to, and tell me the old stories, tell me
everything written down in that bright book: everyone here has
    a thread
of the story, we need to braid them into a river.

Down on the road she turns and her eyes are shining:
eyes of a dancing daughter, a youngest sister, eyes of a mother,
her gaze giving back the clear eyes of her beautiful daughters,
the clear, mischievous eyes of our beloved Aunt —

and far back where her eyes are bright as river pebbles
I see the tall pipe major who gave her, at once and forever, his
    whole heart.
We close around him in a solid phalanx and she smiles, who
    loved him so.
A lone swan beats through the air above the river, catching
    the light.

Midsummer, the road opening down into the valley,
the laughing girl on the road, walking away from the world
and down there in the trees, by the bridge over the river,
all of us with our arms thrown wide in welcome.

i.m. Angela Dorgan O'Connell 1931–2011

Learning My Father's Memories

I saw Cúchulainn in his latter years,
great knots of muscle in his shoulders,
the gleaming dome of his skull in the afternoon.

I saw him drive younger warriors from the field
by the fierce power of his eye on the frozen ball,
his gift for gathering and unleashing force.

He fought each autumn match through a fog of glories
already legend, the air he prowled in doubled,
and his step doubled with a younger self.

I saw his last matches for The Glen, the young bucks
already impatient to sweep him to the heavens
where blood and raw knuckles, mud and defeat

or victory would fade into remembered youth —
a child myself, I sensed their insensate cruelty,
the watchful precise impatience of the young.

Powerful because legend, his powers already fading,
each match by then a match with himself only,
the grammar of ageing played out in the Mardyke mud.

Christ, he was younger then than I am now!
My father's age, who seemed so old to me then,
and now so young. So it goes on, the old parade

through sweat and mud and memory, the hero,
his followers and his fellow warriors ...
And back there on the grass-banked terrace

a round-eyed child in his own fog of doubt,
testing the fix in a spin of words and meanings:
"That's him, I'm looking at him, Christy Ring."

The Angel of Days to Eugene Lambert

And what did you do on earth?

I did my work.

I went at it all wide-eyed,
with a steady heart.
I reared strong sons and daughters,
I mastered my craft.

And what was the best of it?

Loving, and being loved.

I pity God, who never walked home by night
or drove the length of Ireland in the rain,
or came in from the workshop
with a new story, sawdust and glue on his hands,
to Mai in the full house — such a welcome I had!

And what would you have changed?

Nothing. Not one blessed thing.

I loved my world —
the hush when a story started up,
watching my hands at work,
children, their laughter.
I never minded the black days —
storms will blow over, it's their nature.

And what will you do now?

It's been a long road, I might have a rest.
I might do a small bit of work, to keep my hand in.

i.m. Eugene Lambert 1928–2010

Going to the Chateau

Happiness today was a field ablaze with poppies.
Tomorrow we are going to see the Chateau. — D.M.

Listen, my darling, listen: the wind going over.
That dry green meadow down there below,
I'm watching it come and go, the way your look does,
going out to the horizon then settling
on my neck. My long hair blowing free.
You draw on a cigarette, taking me in.
That way you have, so many years now.

The best I had of this life was in your look,
through smoke dancing as a door blew open, or
walking down Wellington Road in the early morning,
climbing that *via Dolorosa* in winter rain.
Your eyes catching mine sometimes black points of fire,
more often so deep going in and seeing me
I would catch my breath. I was a stranger
wandering this earth until I found home with you.

Everything that we ever did was right.
Everywhere that we walked, lay, climbed or swam
was a spur and nurture to curiosity,
your virtuoso flourishes with the brush
or mine in dyes a kind of guarantee —
invocation of the world when it's being itself.

Sweetheart, stretch out your arms, and let your eye
be dry and exact now as it ever was,
look a last time on these my bones.

Place poppies on my breast, measure me.
make me a bed of silence to be my home.

Oh, bring me home.

But first we are going to see the famous Chateau.
Are you afraid? Don't be, I knew you wouldn't be.
Take my hand, be shy again with me, be strong,
now more than ever, and I will carry your look
with me to the door. Breathe in my mouth
and press my lips, my poppy lips. Remember me,
such a rich and true life as we made,
be proud of me as I have been proud of you,
remember these poppies, this lush, darkening field,
this cold oncoming starry rush of night.

i.m. Deirdre Meaney, artist, 1948–1999

Prayer to the Mothers of Rain

Send down your sweet
cascading rain
on all who burn;
wrap them in sea mist
& gather them to the pool.
Deluge their upturned faces,
oh let fall
cataract, sheet rain,
torrent of cold water

that their bones may cool,
their furnace hearts fall quiet,
that dry rage cease.

May they find peace who are in fire
wreathed and bound,
oh bring them on home in your
song of water.
You who were daughters once,
now mothers forever,
send down your rain,
your cold, consoling rain.

i.m. Paula McCarthy, 1957–2001

Nine for the Nine Bright Shiners

1.

A dead boy stands under a falling ball,
gathering the future in its downward rush,
a blank sputnik plunging to earth,
and the wind buffeting his face
is the wind of the world without him,
January wind of the world when he has gone.
The night rattles my window and he stands on the green
outside, a city he never stood in, the ball still falling,
a winter moon full in the sky,
and a wind from the moon sweeps the dead boy away, away —
friend of my childhood how hot our blood was,
how springy and clean our breathing and our bones.
Now I am stiff and tired and cold. And you are not.

2.

You were dying for days in our city by the river,
lost at night, I'm sure of it, in a metal bed so close
to home— so far, oh much too far. Was there a bird
battling the window with its wings? I see a bird.
London's police, two numbers, three addresses,
height of the Irish troubles, they couldn't find me.
A Paddy with three addresses, two numbers.
You couldn't find me. Oh the cold clarity going home.
Phone, train tickets and plane, everyone standing back,
I was a travelling man of ice but your blood no sun
would ever warm again. Everyone said I looked taller —
it was will, straight-backed implacable cast of grief.
Did you die believing I knew but would not come?

3.

Fog on the playing field, late evening; we make a line
and sweeping the lank grass with our hurleys we cross
from one side to the other, searching for what is lost.
Now we are cold as sweat dries on our backs, our legs
are blue, our breath staggered and wispy in the air.
The line advances, year by year it advances towards
the deep ditch where, one by one, if the earth endures,
in time they will find our bones. I raise my head up
and find myself still out there in that line,
beating the grass in a fury, such a waste of time.
I see the long file stretch out across the field,
gaps in the ranks already, uncertain men where
once there were boys who would downface Alexander.

4.

Never had much to say for himself, Billy.
Teachers walked carefully around him, sensing the edge
on that considered silence, fearing that hooded look.
Evenings he'd walk the river with a book;
Zen poems, I remember, once on Lavitt's Quay
when our orbits crossed, myself a solitary by then,
my mind shot through with intimate doubts and fears.
I don't remember what we said,
but after that he'd nod if we met by chance
and I would feel steadied, a moment less unsure.
He chose a dead-end job, with care I see now,
then drank himself steadily young to death.
Somebody told me, by the river. Just walked in.

5.

Something possessed him in those last years,
some contrary spirit that had him loving to new friends,
bitter deliberate enemy to the old.
Eyes that had burned with hunger burned with cold.
Frail boy, faint ghost of Trotsky, riven by need
to be and speak, how did we not see such greed for life
would turn in the roil of drink and baffled fury
to blunt fear of what he once was? Something untoward
had uncoiled in his blood, some worm or gall
had bled into the ink, but we who stood wounded,
taken aback, what was our fault? He feared to freeze when faced
with fire, the long climb back to zero if he should fail.
We should have known, no man will face Calvary again.

6.

One or another of my aunts, your daughters, told us the story:
how you had your sons climb on the kitchen table and jump
on your promise you'd catch them. Let that be a lesson,
you told the bewildered boys, never trust anyone,
not even your father. Your own mother sent overboard
at Cape Horn, your first breath drawn in these dark waters.
I stand to the wheel, close-braced inside myself,
a wall of great rollers thundering past, and some deep cold
in me as the Horn recedes; my eyes are wet with salt
but I am unmoved as you were. I see now what made
you do it, I see what you saw. There was love, I do not doubt it,
before and after, but there is a time to see things as they are.
I stand on into the long night beside you, shoulder to shoulder.

7.

So serious, we would say, until she smiled
from under her black fringe and the child
flashed through the woman who was to be.
While *Maman* worked she'd shop and cook,
serious and self-contained; she could command
her sharp twin brother with a look. A dancer,
never still if she could help it, but a book
would fold her into silence. That winter she turned twelve,
as we were turning out into separate lives.
Once, out of the darkness, her soft voice:
"Qu'est ce que vous faites, Maman?" "On fait l'amour."
A small, reflective silence, then: *"J'ai envie."*
The fates would cut her thread at seventeen.

8.

The gas man flicks coins from the table into his cupped palm,
a blur of copper and silver. He stacks neat columns to one side,
we like that something is returned. We like this man.
Today he stands at the top of the steps, side by side with my
    father,
they are looking down and away into the stepped valley,
not speaking now, watching someone swing brisk down Water
    Lane.
I am turning over *pneumonia, pleurisy, septic lungs* and they turn
to look at me. A new word, sudden and clear: *Pity.* I say it
    silently.
Like the other words. Small, hard polished things. *Nuala,* I say,
    Nuala.
Somehow it is in my head he will take her away in his leather bag,
our small dead sister; I think this even though she's already away
with the doctor and his leather bag in his shiny, shiny car.
My mother lies in a dark bedroom, staring up at nothing.

9.

We stand for the anthem, buoyant and tribal, heart beating with
    heart,
our colours brave, our faces turned from the uncertain sun.
The man beside me takes my hand, good luck to yours, he says;
I squeeze his calloused palm and then — he's gone.
A shadow socket where he was, the one beside him vanishes
and another before me, behind me; all around Croke Park
one by one we wink out of existence: tens, hundreds, then
thousands, the great arena emptying out, the wind curling in
from the open world to gather us all away. Each single one of us.
I could feel myself fail at the end, but then maybe everyone
    thought that,
each one of us the last to go. The whistle blew and we all
came back with a roar, everything brighter and louder, desperate
    and vivid.
I held his hand a moment longer, I wished his team all the luck
    in the world.

Café

In the entire boom and confusion
of the café, one point of stillness:
a man reading over and over
the last letter received from his dead father.

Learning Death

The first time I knew myself mortal,
that unmistakable catch in the breath,
we were new to each other still.
I was stroking your face as you sank
towards sleep, and said without meaning to:
call me if you need me over there.

Full moonlight, the square white bedroom,
your eyes startling open, aftershock
in the cold air of what I had just said.
The crackling electric thought we took,
one breath between us, so close we lay —
how matter of fact that was, how clear.

And there we were, borne up on a void
soundlessly opened, shy with each other,
stricken all of a sudden to know time
might contrive to part us against our will.
I knew what mortal meant: you might call
and I would not be there for you — grief

worse than any I had felt, my life until then.
Now, facing the white blank of the page,
that thought again, unbidden: there will be
an end to words, an end to compact, breath —
you shaped my face in your hands, you said:
"You'll be there. I'll be there." And we slept.

That Look Again

The traveller woman on Baggot Street
is arguing with Michael Hartnett's ghost,
her stabbing hands make gestures in the folds
of her wool shawl that I can't read.
Her mouth is moving twisted but her eyes
are black with fire and do not blink.
The pressure in my chest now so intense
that I am half afraid to breathe.

The morning sun is cold and hard, the light
so sharp I catch the gleam of teeth
when Michael bows and smiles and lifts his cap
then looks down shyly at his feet.
The passersby, oblivious, go shuffling past,
a shoulder-awkward stream;
this pocket of null quiet is here — then gone,
a self-cancelling moment in a dream.

The boom of traffic buffets us, the windows
flash a semaphore of cloud,
the trees above our heads are heavy laden
with their cargoes of green cold;
everything and everyone is washed and
pushed about by this dry gale.
Now Michael turns upon his heel,
salutes the woman backward, walks away.

The wind dips and lifts me to roof height.
I hang there, at peace, thoughtful and cold.
Everything stops.
I look down on her eyes, beads of black fire.
Michael's eyes, looking up and back.

Michael, Michael

Michael, I was on the East Link in a taxi when the nurse
in my ear said, soft and sad, I'm afraid your friend is dead.

A wind out of Munster shook the bridge.

We stopped and I stepped to the parapet. October flowed
in the black Liffey below. Ebb tide, by the slanting buoys.

A wind out of Munster shook the bridge.

I closed my eyes, went down and in for Ó Rathaille, Ó Bruadair,
that stiff-eyed company of the living still —

A wind out of Munster shook the bridge.

A wren darted from hedge to hedge and they followed it
with their eyes, hands lifted in welcome —

A wind out of Munster shook the bridge.

The wren became a wraith became a stately air,
turned in the bony hands of a watchful piper.

A wind out of Munster shook the bridge.

What shall we do for timber ? The last of the woods are down
and our quiet master down. I got back in, we drove to the toll.

A wind out of Munster shook the bridge.

The driver paid and asked was I all right, would we go on?
Drive on, I said, drive on. He was a good man.

And the wind behind us shook the bridge.

Mirror

The mirror cracked
from top to bottom
and he walked through;

the wind gone south
between full moon and no moon,
that's when we hear him sing.

In Glasnevin Cemetery

The ground is heavy clay, the weighted spade
a live thing in my grip as I cut the ground.
Pale sky, pale rushing clouds, a brother's hands
sifting your father's ashes on your mother's grave.

Your sisters stand and watch, their lovely daughters
gathered in close as this one last time you grant him
a daughter's gesture: here's Rosemary, for remembrance
(I open a cup of ground as you bed it in)

here's wallflowers (you sift in compost, pat the ground firm)
tough and tenacious as any Dub — and I am struck,
shook, to think what I owe this man I loved,
this woman I never met, laid in the one grave.

We finish the work, I spade the earth neat and flat;
you rise from your crouch, a hand in the small of your back.
Her eyes, his eyes in your look, the twin dark stars
that struck me spellbound the day we met.

And so life goes on, borne down on the wind —
I am thinking this as I heft the spade and turn
to walk away, no longer sure what, if anything, I believe,
until your small strong hand takes a grip of mine.

Clay and ash on the wind, on our shoes; high clouds,
a keen cold wind, your sisters' laughter, their daughters
stepping clear — your father and mother in the wind
and one day, my love, we two in the wind —

What of it? The wind blows from always to always,
and didn't you tell me once, and didn't I tell you,
this is for always, the wind and whoever spins it
and we two borne up on it beyond the grave?

On a Day Far From Now

Death will come and have your eyes
and I will go into her arms
without fear or hesitation.

Frost on the slates
of our beloved square,
the cars riding low under
a hurrying sky when

I open the great hall door
and take her hand,
her long black coat.

The bare-flagged hallway, frost
and perfume on the night air.

I watch her let down
her gleaming hair,
open her slender arms
in your exact gesture.

Death will come and have your eyes
and I will go into her arms
alone and unafraid.

after a line by Cesare Pavese

Chorus

He Spins a Story

He spins a story like a man peeling a fruit,
the tale spilling from his hands like orange rind.

Even his silences are noted — transcribed by biographers
with sticks borrowed from the blind.

The ears of his audience being all of an equal size,
let *them* work it out, let *them* sort true from false —
and hang truth from the rafters with plaits of garlic,
tossing the scraps to the dogs, to the beggars at the wall.

The listening women are filling their jugs with his words
before pouring them into their beds until they shimmer in flame,
they are certain he will keep talking until the sun burns itself out.

translated from the French of Venus Khoury Ghata

She Travels in Winter

Oh set her down safe for me, what care have I other?
God of the upper air, new fears are sprung in me,
hung on the wall stark blank before me here tonight.
Let her not down plummet wrapped in sheets of thunder,
be smashed from air this night of winter's wrath over
O'Hare, Chicago, spun out into the mid west nightblack,
by storm and by ice be hurled, howled under, spun —
who is best of my life here, comrade hereafter sworn
as now and for years; silent by fire with me,
bent into wind by shore wracked in her mystery,
or brilliant, the morning's glory in her face,
as once when new she bathed me all in her grace.

Such morning I wish her now, down, safe, cosseted
and smooth in some heated terminal, phone in hand,
to say: love, it was rough but something brought us through.
What, and down safe you set her, would I not do for you?

The Child I Was Regards the Infinite

Tilted, a great plain, over Water Lane and the valley below
or flexed in the long green matrix of that hedge
where he'd sit and breathe the evening light of summer,
feeling the emptiness as a physical ache.

At night deep space was bracked with flickering stars
and the silence over the Bishop's Field went all the way
up forever into the blank vault of fear.
Street lights below, the stars above, between them the beyond.

The wind had edges would tip and tune your mind
out past familiar voices to the pitch of keening,
a fear like that you felt in the year's new classroom,
the dull boom of damnation in a black soutane.

And here I stand, I tell myself now, here where these memories
are jagged rocks of glass, the sea washing over, falling away,
no more sure of anything than that child ever was
but stubborn still, willing to face it all down for eternity.

after Giacomo Leopardi's 'l'Infinito'

Insomnia

Because I could not catch my breath
I thought that I must die —
Grief had carried off the Bridge
from you to I.

The torrent carried down the cage
that Thought had made — the sky
like wreckage turned in that full flood
from you to I.

The morning broke against the glass
— let Mind and Nature fly—
And I had made that Span again
from you to I.

Solace

I lie on my stomach
on the earth:

I draw up
damp and cold
for my bones,

dry heat
for my veins,

the calm & peace
of substance
for my thought.

version from the Slovenian of Barbara Korun

Song of Mis at the Winter Solstice

Nights of hard frost
in the holy tree
trapped like a bird
with wetfrozen feathers
I'd lay myself down in a sheet of ice
my feet sticking out,
frost potatoes
on long withered stalks,
and sing morning's canticle;
hagridden, trembling
on the drone of hope,
frost of morning hardening again,
my pulse of song
freezing and falling
into bitter laughter.

I'd be away in a dizzy flight
in mad career
in springing leaps
from elm to yew
harrowing myself on spines of blackthorn,
half-crazy
the people thought,
only that
deep in my marrow,
deep between marrow and bone,
between the lunatic madness
and the madness of a sane woman
memory was nesting, brooding,
sputtering with damp heat …

One morning, grief-struck in the chapel yew,
frost-flowers on my eyes,
spine in locked spasm,
hammering
on frozen tree trunk,
my red-raw buttocks
discharging
a froth, a scutter of watercress,
I turned to the east
and a gleam of sunlight kissed my eyes,
a glitter of sunlight melted the ice in my look.

A long finger of light traced
the curve of my lips,
stroked my raw cheekbones,
rested on my cheek.

I felt the black grief thaw in my heart,
light lancing the poisoned wound,
the dark running out of me;
I stretched my hands out to the sun
as it reddened the clouds,
as it picked out, lit up, flake after flake of snow —
until earth and air became a sea of light
that carried my heart to harbour.

In the deep of every winter since,
in the dark entrails of the year,
in return for this grace and favour
I set the sun up in my heart,
I lance it high into the bowl of air and light
on a bolt of music,
that the birds may follow it into the mouth of spring.

translated from the Irish of Biddy Jenkinson

In Those Days the Earth Was So High ...

In those days the earth was so high
that women would hang out clouds and washing on the one line
— prudent angels would grab them by the skirts
lest they fly away after lost souls.

The word *soul* was given to anything that touched water —
jugs, pots, ladles, gourds —
buckets were used to retrieve all who languished in deep wells,

every moving shadow was an exquisite revenant,
every cock–crow an omen.

The Announcer of Birds in the valley spoke louder than the
      waterfall
but softer than the wind that roared inside and out;
she swept the horizon back an acre all around,

swelling the little fields,
shrinking the house to a birdcage
so that the nightingale keep its pride.

Better not met by the wayside,
she'd break a man over her knee the way you'd snap a straw.

translated from the French of Venus Khoury Ghata

The Love Poems of Lena Stakheyeva

1.

There was a room, once, with red curtains,
our hands were stained with love
like blackberry juice;
we will never know such pain again.

Planes of light tilt in the room,
the train far off
groans on the brake.

We turn from the window
to the floor of what is sure.
Wind, rain, what should we care?
The door opens on sad violins, bangs shut.

2.

It is not enough to love, but it is necessary.
Four birches, a railed fence, a meadow.
The sea beneath us folded in heavy bronze.

3.

Four corners pillar the room,
the floorboards flinch from time,
the furniture shrinks from the light,
the coal fire is plain.

4.

You kissed my cheek, a stone wave
broke in my breath, fell back.
You closed the door quietly, it clicked.
Your step went slowly down the stairs.

5.

A single car parked on the square, snow,
a scribble of footprints. Voices like gunshots —
somebody learning that love begins in light,
goes through the dark, comes out in light again.

6.

There is a way to walk & breathe,
and I have forgotten it.
You turned up the music,
walked to the window, stood there.

7.

Ignore the way home, strike out
that defended line, watch
how the cat threads in and out the fence.
Sure and certain, captain of the dark.

8.

I forget now what shoes you wore,
but your feet were cold and wet.
I brought you a towel from
deep in the cupboard —
from its open wings the summer flew out,
swooped to caress your feet.

9.

Turn down the music,
let the violins fade now,
let guitars & smokefilled voices
fill up the room.

Pull the red curtains closed;
kindness is sudden and sure,
a gift of winter roses.
Your ivory shoulders
a crescent against the night;
the dark stars of your look
soften to human. A ship fades
down the sighing river, I spell
the word *blessed* in letters of your name.
We possess ourselves again.

What Wonders

Oh Mr. Bones I tell you it is hell,
to love, and love well, and be not desired.

But Henry, Henry, at our age love is grim,
moment by moment face to face with death,
facing eternity in the here and now,
waking in panic not to hear her breath.
We love, and lie there as the light grows dim
holding the well-loved other back from death.
What would I, waking, breathing here and now
not give, the half of what once I would get
for blood as hot as yours? You have it yet,
the pulse of life that I now half forget.
Desire? The body kindling to time's glow?
Henry! This life we have is touch and go.

The Choice

I watched Odysseus go on board the flagship
and moved to follow, but something took hold of me.
I turned my back on the business of campaigning,
all of a sudden sick of captaincy, of voyaging;

I turned for the sunlit uplands, my olives and vine farms,
the quiet of purple evenings, and never once looked back.

I might have died at sea, worn out by empty longing,
smashed in the neck with a bronze axe or drowned —
and for what? To have grown old in someone's story,
shade of a warrior with no issue in family or the earth?

I chose silence, the turning of verses, the struggle with words.
Did he do better, wrapped in his fate, when he chose swords?

The Senator, on the Feast of Saturn, to his Friend Serving in Sicily, 217 BCE

Last night I dreamed, and this is what I dreamed:

Blood and rough wine in the sand
the sandal beating the sand
and blood on the dancer's hands
the rough wine drenching her hair

And the beacons lit on the promontories
the old gods in the wood by the shore
the bronze axe in the block
and the flat stone where the god stood

The stars in their ancient courses
and the old gods in the wood turning away
and the dancers linking hands
dipping and swaying in the onshore wind

The ships drawn up on the beach
the campfire of driftwood and cedar
the sailors oiling their dark curls
and laughing with bare-breasted girls

The black bread dipped in wine
passing from hand to hand, from mouth to mouth
and the words of the proper song:
Cronos, youngest of Titans, Cronos...

Whom we, Gaius, appropriate as Saturn,
whose festival we have today decided
must stretch to a week — to appease the people,

to distract them from this crushing defeat
at the hands of the Carthaginians.

Statecraft demands it of us, that what we find
we must bend to the good of the Republic,
that good we alone are charged to ordain.
Order is everything, order and decorum;
thus, for a week, no more, we permit this licence.

You there in Sicily, old friend, do not forget Rome,
but do not forget what we sacrifice to duty —
the old gods who have not gone away,
those nights when we thought ourselves youngest of Titans.

The Sea, The Sea

Setting Out

The night is breathing soft and dark,
I'm slipping away on the ebb tide,
easing the mainsheet, letting go —
an ear cocked for the far-off thud of surf.
Sirius down to starboard, steady as Venus,
the night shimmers around me,
a black scribble of wake runs aft,
folds, catches the starlight, falls away.

I am writing us both out on the page of night,
and under this, under all, beating below-decks
and beating ahead, a boom in a sea-cave,
a trick of the rising wind,
the soft thump, thump of your heart,
the heart in my ribcage, my heart in your breast,
pulse of seaway, pulse of the iodine dark,
warm pulse of night, sleep.

Love, whatever the morning brings —
if we reach that shore —
whatever light pales, falls and steadies
in foam scrawled on the dawn-wet sand,
let the throb in the timbers,
the pulse in the sail and the keel,
be always your heart, my heart,
the heart of our one and only world.

And let the light flare and the tall sail fill and catch,
let the drums of the world beat on, on and forever

Now it is night, night breathing soft and dark,
I am slipping away on the ebb,
easing the main, letting go;
I keep an ear to the drumming of surf,
the night shimmering all around us now;
it folds you warm in sleep, glinting with dreams,
safe down below in trust, steady and sure.
I stand to the helm, hold to the fated course.

It Was Him All Right

Making north for Kinsale out of the Azores,
a fresh breeze at dawn, alone at the helm,
I was checking all around me,
tending the mainsheet, listening to Mozart's *Requiem*
and there he was on the coachroof,
a tailor considering where to chalk his cut.

His back and head erect, his shoulders bowed,
diffident, certain, reticent and proud.

Tailor, indeed, or some slight seagoing demon,
he sat there a moment, lifted that neat-eared head
and looked right through me. We fell off a wave
and I almost gybed, the shock running up
through the mast as I fought back the wheel.
A roar from below: Are you all right?

Gone when I looked up, spun back into the track.
That fleet to starboard, making on for the fall of Munster.

In the Here and Now

She dips to the swell,
curves under and comes
up, wash of white water
coursing back her decks.

This could be any boat,
but is this boat, now:
clawing North, alive,
climbing for westerlies.

Staysail & mainsail pinned in hard;
something is passing through
two days ahead, sending this lucky wind,
this leftover swell.

I look away forward,
the helm under my hand
alive in the moment.
Her keel parts the water

cleanly, again, and again,
her bow dips and rises —
she's found a rhythm,
sailing herself today.

Somebody's making coffee below —
Charlotte, she's up next.
I draw the wake-furrow clean,
canted to starboard, wind in the north west.

Watchkeeping

The crew sleep on, my care for now,
so different each from each.
Zafer, going down, says casually:
"Just keep us off the beach."
Dry in their bunks they dream
beyond the long swell's reach.

A lee shore on the port bow,
storm petrels, what they teach.
Thunder ashore and a lowering sky,
I am well beyond speech,
all concentration. Wind coming up,
tighten the mainsail leech.

Here is what helming is, and trust:
we rest or we take the watch, we do what we must.

At Midnight We Raised the Fastnet

Twenty miles on a clear night, fitful stars.
So many other lights to reckon with,
trawlers, an east-bound coaster, something
we weren't sure of going away from us
on the same course. Simon, calm
at the helm, picking them out one by one.

It should have been cold, we had come so far north,
and I was tired but couldn't go below.
Coming home off the sea, perhaps that was it,
or a kind of doubling with my grandfather's ghost —
seeing him now as the newborn child he was.
I hold that child up, first sight of his homeland,
I hold his beloved son, my father, suddenly as close.

There, up ahead, my mother to welcome us home —
all blazed in light, confident, beautiful, young.

Gaffer

She loomed up out of the near-dusk, quiet,
long-keeler, gaff ketch, maybe fifty
yards off on the same course, loping along,
hullwash sibilant on her faded sides.
I roared at the crew in temper:
where did he come from, there on the lee?
What kind of watch are ye keeping?
Everyone looked away, I sounded unfair.
Ducked my head back inside,
could see nothing on radar.

Hailed him, the solitary man at the wheel,
He turned to look at us,
tilted the brim of his cap,
stared off ahead again.
The wind was fresh, I had a reef in
but he was carrying full sail, kerosene
running lights in his rigging, flare
of his port light a flame on the faded mainsail.
I took him for English, out of Dorset or Cornwall.

He flew no flag but everything there before us
spoke of an earned authority,
ease, the absence of doubt. For maybe an hour
he held station there beside us,
never again cast a glance in our direction.
Full dark came on, we shook out the reef
and pulled ahead — light displacement, fin-keel,
the boat barely two years old. I wanted more
from this encounter than I could grasp,
had sand in my brain, some mind's infection.

We were bound for Kinsale but off the Sovereigns
something came over me, a sudden desire to be inside.
We made in for Oysterhaven, picked up a mooring
and settled for the night. Over the thick wooded
south ridge, a sky of stars stood up.
I sat there smoking while down below
was laughter, a burr of voices, a rattle of pans.
Somebody's mobile rang, strident and wrong.

"Where do you think he is now?" Rob, coming up.
We turned to the scribble of surf
in the harbour mouth, half-expecting that blunt sail
to blank the cottage lights. He must be staying out,
I said, making on for the west.
The last red overhead faded,
a land breeze came up, smelling of leafmould.
Rob rapped the coachroof with a knuckle, looked out
and away, said "Forecast is good, he'll be okay."
I don't suppose, I said, the weather bothers him.

Skellig: Sailing to the Edge

1.

A sail on the horizon,
make it two,
rags of cloud at the truck;
(the rise and fall,
the south wind)
slow moving,
both hull-down.

We tend ship,
haul fenders in,
coil dripping lines;
we settle
to the swell,
dispose ourselves,
seek shelter
from the wind.

I look again:
not sails but
island peaks,
deep-rooted
in deep water,
the tide sweeps
past their bows;
we slant off south.

Cormorants,
gannets, shags,
shearwaters,

petrels, gulls —
we make for
a cloud of souls
swept upward
into cloud.

2.

Chug of the diesel, water slop in bilge.
the boatman throttles back a hint,
we dip to the swell. We settle.

Who made out first from Portmagee
for these black peaks, what hull
danced under him, what was in his mind?

For now I don't care, happy to be at sea,
braced to the lift and fall, at home out here.
I turn my phone off, unscrew the thermos, drink.

3.

Province of sword and fire, of lust for land —
and that other province, of minds hungry for God,

for first and last things, far horizons.
One interweaved in the other, a riddle unpicked

when strong-minded abbots sailed
to build Christ's citadel on a rock.

Michael for patron, prince of angels, warrior saint.
An island fortress on the world's edge.

4.

We land on the surge, the boatman wrestling the wheel,
the mass of rock looms over us, solid and black.

One element for another; mocked by the wheeling gulls,
we climb heavy-footed into air. Salt on my sleeve

when I pause to wipe my brow, shale & samphire at my feet.
Weight presses us from beneath, pushing through lungs,

opening us out until we stand clear on the North Peak.
Down there and out, and out again, the sea and the sea beyond.

Simple as that. We stoop and step inside, taking it all in —
the limestone pavement, the wells, the corbelled huts —

made thoughtful, of course, impressed, but also elsewhere.
The elsewhere that is eternal here and now.

5.

Coptic or Greek or native Irish, what would it matter
to that black cormorant falling past like a thunderbolt?

The sun blazes out over far hills and valleys,
there in that lost place beyond the sea

where fathers and mothers and homes are no more than dreams,
where a child, dawdling home, sees two sails far out to sea.

The sun blazes on overhead although there's a storm coming —
the boatman earlier, tracking its advent, said

magicseaweed.com is the best of prophets —
the sun blazes down on us from the blank future,

circled by souls from the living past,
gleams on the wind, spume in our eyes.

6.

We climb to the South Peak, privileged, on ropes,
belayed on each steep pitch, alive to danger,

and there on the high hermitage we turn to the west,
fearing to see God knows what. Beneath us, cliff edge,

a ledge of prayer. Monks would kneel here,
hands uplifted, for hours, days on end.

Fulmars and petrels barrel past, scanting the wind.
That ancient, light-packed trope — the soul as bird.

7.

The swell's come up, the boat home edges in.
The black wall recedes in a wash of surf.

We heel, and then we're tide-borne, steady,
making out solid and sure for haven, home.

Layers of paint on the thwart, the wheelhouse, hot in the sun.
The chill comes on quickly as the wind picks up.

The cove opens its arms to us, we turn in,
butting the rising waves, the offshore chop.

The wind's come up, keening then deepening to a roar,
fading away until some remembered sorrow calls it back.

I feel it in my bones: tonight under the low cliff
will be growl and suck of surf, pounding,

the ground under the house shook —
the boatman knows, I catch it in his look.

Behind us the islands have turned north,
sailing into the wind now, wind from the land of cold.

Walls of Green Water

1.

Walls of green water overtopped with white,
a grey surge under, bearing the weight up
until it topples, gaining speed, and a big sea
thunders across the afterdeck.

day after day of this

Wind under all, great thunder in the sails,
hard to believe they stand so tall
under all that strain, that the mast
can stand the constant blast and sway.

day after day of this

We plough on, rising and falling to the swell,
deep under now, the bow now rearing high
out of a welter of green water, the howl
in the rigging shivering our bones.

day after day of this

Clouds shredding past like rags of catastrophe,
Justin stands to the wheel in the glass bright light,
all of his body-weight lead in his feet,
all counter-sway and balance, feeding the helm.

day after day of this

Hands jammed in pockets, braced to the rise and fall,
Kevin surveys the horizon, reading the wind,
the swell, the waves — the turbulent music of the day.
Cold sluice over the wheelhouse, he ducks and laughs.

day after day of this

Walls of green water overtopped with white,
a grey surge under, bearing the weight up
until it topples, gaining speed, and a big sea
thunders across the afterdeck.

day after day of this

Tony, inside, tugs at his cuff — a flash of wristwatch.
Time for the log entry: date, time, course and speed,
the meticulous pencilled *X* that says, on the wide expanse of chart,
we are here. Now. We have come this far.

day after day of this

The off watch are tumbled in their bunks, so many bodies
braced against crash and fall, down in the dark
where thought and feeling meld, cushioned in meat and blood
against bone-crack, exhaustion, the howl of the wind.

day after day of this

I buckle up: lifejacket, safety line, harness. Time to go out,
to check for chafe, lost shackles, anything that's not right.
Sixty five knots of wind, up to the bow and back.
One hand for yourself, one hand for the ship.

day after day of this

Albatross in the backdraft from the mainsail
hangs in the air, banks slowly, settles back
to its long stately progress through white light.
It hangs in air we breathe through haze and spray.

day after day, still doubled with her ghost.

2.

She died in childbirth off Cape Horn, great grandmother,
died on a black ship heading home, the deck plunging and rising,
the air down below fetid and chill. Salt everywhere,
sweat in her hair and eyes, her breath faltering, falling still.

There at the end of the world, her house of memory caving in,
in lamplight, maybe, or in weak daylight failing, the cold,
it would have been cold, her fear for the child, the ebb
in her blood, her last thought a nurse for the child.

The board on the lee rail, her body on it, wrapped in old canvas,
lead weights at her feet. Good men to shoulder the board,
the Captain intoning the service, his words on the wind.
If it were me I'd have done it at night, under the Southern Cross.

Wait 'til the afterdeck tips to the scudding clouds
then a nod, a sharp tilt and she's over, she slides in
and then it's down, down, down forever into the green dark.
The Book snapped shut. A drink for the men. Everything
        squared away.

3.

We work the boat, we ride the thundering wind,
we brace to the lift and fall, we do whatever's needed,
we do more when we can. When we fall into sleep the others rise,
they stand in to their duty. The boat drives on.

Day after day, still doubled with her ghost, I dream or work
and somehow it's all the same to me, the sea, my dreams,
the wind, my father, boom of the hull breaking a wave,
my grandfather's pale eyes — all the one plunging vortex.

We plough on, rising and falling to the swell,
deep under now, the bow now rearing high
out of a welter of green water,
the howl in the rigging shivering our bones.

Now and forever, waking or sleeping,
in the only world there is,
under flying clouds by day,
under flashing stars by night,
now and forever
borne up and out and on,
crashing through walls of green water,
we drive on, we drive on,
we hold to our mortal course.

House of Echoes

Nine Instances of Grace

1.

That time in Vienna, the Kunsthistorisches Museum,
when you drifted off into a landscape
by Pieter Bruegel the Elder

Or the night on the aft upper deck
of the ferry to Lesvos
when you drifted out over the wake

Or that time last week, in the garden,
when the Brent Geese came over
and you drifted up into the sun?

You had snow on your collar,
you had salt on your cheek,
you had gold in your eyes —

And each time I stretched out my hand, silent,
and you of your own volition came plummeting back.

2.

The plane floats in, roar of reverse thrust,
the flaps come up, a bump,
another and we're down.

I should have kept count,
so many flights since that first
lift into the air together,

so many landings in so many places.
How lucky we've been,
to drink the air, to bathe in water

all over our beloved world,
to see this earth together,
me through your eyes, you through mine,

mimosa and dust of villages, city diesel,
again and again the lift and plunge into the blue.

3.

How you are often in two places at once —
today, for instance, the cliff road to Agios Kirikos,
rapt in some random visitation

you glance back, an eyebrow climbing over
whatever you're going to say and I realize
you're on a road in Leitrim with your friends.

I wonder how Pat and Peter are, I say; your grin
as bright as the sea below, your knowing
there's no need to speak of this,

how a thought forming in your mind
will shape in mine, how my hand
reaching forward to tap you on the shoulder

will meet your hand reaching back.
How we walk on, our fingers intertwined.

4.

Night. We climb the hill past sleeping oleanders.
We come to those interwoven tamarisks
wrapped around a streetlight,

and then the long curve where they quarried,
where loose rock carries down still to the road.
Full moon on your shoulder when I look at you,

then the sudden glow on the ridge above Therma,
flame climbing the far side of the mountain ahead.
The sea beneath us glitters, the scant lights of the village

in the bowl below are steady, the quiet untroubled.
We imagine fire crossing the saddle, roaring down
in a torrent on Agriolykos, our present home —

they'd be out of their beds by now, you say.
I was thinking the same thing. We walk on down.

5.

The feral tabby, the village cat you call Pangur Bán,
is more than usually agitated, curving between
the rickety chairs, urgent and morning-plaintive.

The milk pan is coming to the boil, the coffee roast
is wreathed in and out with near-done toast,
the daily circus is getting into gear and here's me,

half clown, half acrobat, saving the toast and pouring
from shoulder height into the milk (you like the froth)
somehow contriving also to feed the cat.

You surface out of a white cloud, nose first as usual,
hunting the tang of coffee; then your eyes open,
your marvellous, lucent bluegrey eyes. You squint,

suspicious: You look awfully smug today ... do I hear the cat?
I magic toast, yoghurt, an orange, out of thin air.

6.

The rustle of carob leaves, brittle even when green,
a small breeze down from the Aetheros, tentative
and sly. Down below, corrugations on the water.

Such a ramshackle village, rust bleeding through walls,
dust everywhere, clapped-out cars, a scurf of dead leaves
on the beach; a clang up the valley, pipes being fitted.

Not sly, just shy. The breeze dips and dandles the branches
of carob and olive, tamarisk and oak, testing the coming season
as I walk the terrace, weighing the half-wrought line.

Around the corner, Samos on your horizon,
I know without looking you're at your table
under the venerable mastic, a pen in your hand.

April in Ikaria, hum of a fishing boat, pulse of work.
Far back, and far away, the house of the winds.

7.

How without needing to talk we set to work.
You get the broom, start quartering the terrace,
neat crescents of leaves driven before you.

I get the hose, shake out a winter's kinks, connect it.
Tea, I think, temper the work; I put the kettle on.
I savour the taste of light sweat on your brow. Then your hip

tipped to one side, to bump on mine as you take the cup.
This quiet now, shoulder to shoulder, the broom at our feet,
as we gaze on a season's wrack, the stirrings of spring.

Where did we learn such silence, earn these deep breaths?
As well ask where the carob learned to make its tight flowers,
where the sea beneath learned to flow without moving.

I spin the tap, cold water rushes through and blurs the air,
the mist glinting like diamonds in your hair.

8.

You paint the world in water, leaning over
a bockety table of tacked-together wood,
the terrace between us as the day fails.

Evening comes on with a rush.
I pour tea into your favourite blue cup,
standing here at the sink in fading light;

I see the bright clean page as you stand back,
then your sure hand darting in with the brush.
I break the spell, of course: you might falter

without tea. I slide into the silence
with ease of years, zen-influenced devotee
of yours and of whatever shapes the hush.

Slip in and smile, be smiled at, then retreat —
tactful, meticulous, straight-backed and discreet.

9.

I close the file, I save and stand and stretch.
Behind me the deep quiet of your breathing,
a stack of books on the floor between us.

My back aches. I undress as the house ticks on into the dark,
savour the moment as I slip between the sheets —
a neat coda if you don't wake, sign that these bones

have still some remnant of grace, some articulate skill.
Deep down, you wince at my cold feet but rise,
somehow, to plant your hand warm on my neck,

subside, settle a knee across my back.
How our bodies have learned, all these long years, to shift
and accommodate each the other, to speak in sleep.

We give ourselves to the moon-rode shifting tides,
borne up, and on, and out into the night.

Lá Fhéile Bhríde

She spread her green dress
on frosted grass. Blackbird sang.
Crocus, yellow spears.

Five Haiku for You

Seagulls overhead
bank, dip, fall away down wind
they make one bright shape

Look! Short daffodils
the black dog is curious
North wind holds its breath

Bread in the toaster
tea leaves swelling in the pot
chink of two white cups

The shape of your foot
pressed into grains of white sand
world has come inside

Crisp pillows, soft light
you stretch gently, you settle
click — the world expands

The Shelf

I level the brackets, the cast iron birds
you brought from New York, then
balance the board on upturned palms,
set the shelf in place.

Clean timber, resiny, straight in the grain,
clear-sawn, smooth planed.
It sits in the alcove, it floats
head-height in the white kitchen.

I treat myself to a full pot of tea,
pull out a chair and sit there
at the exact centre of the world,
feeling the weight of time in space,

the clean sweet curve it takes
towards the moment you walk in the door;
nursing my satisfaction, savouring
the pleasure you take in simple things, like me.

Night Walk with the Dog, Bella

The tide is going out on the Burrow Beach,
the long murmur, the suck and hiss.
Night, and the islands under the full moon
float at their moorings, nudge and shove.

One of those nights when talk's beyond our reach,
each of us wearing a single glove
the better to hold hands; you scuff your shoes,
the dog carefully watching our every move.

And this is all we need to know of love:
three souls walking the beach,
the tide going out that will come in again,
the dog content, the fated stars above.

Still silent, buoyant, we stop, we turn to kiss
and the black dog goes chasing down the moon.

This Gifted Life

Rain, old veils of winter rain.
The moon come through again.

You walked down the cold iron stairs
sixteen years ago, give or take
a few days, and never walked out.

God knows you threatened to,
driven mad by some obduracy of mine,
some demon from your past,

and as often, my own demons
at my neck, I dreamed of walking out
into some high loneliness of my own.

Let me speak a hard-won truth:
I'd perish without you.

So, let the rain fall; the fire is bright,
the kettle coming to the boil, soon
I'll make tea, we'll settle for the night,

let the phone ring out if it rings,
the life trail out behind us as the world turns.

Here we are, with all the time we will ever need
and nothing to do but work, talk or be silent, as we please.

We'll Go into the Country

Dig out your boots, we'll go into the country,
taking our troubles with us to the air,
far from the milling city, the hard noise
that clogs and cracks our brains.

We'll take our fears and quarrels there,
to that long ridge set out across the sky,
signature on a letter full of doubt,
seismograph of some fall and shock.

Nothing in rock or tree that can't be found
in brick or staircase, but the winds
of mercy do not blow through this city,
there is no soft breath of our mother's voice.

We'll go into the country, my own dear,
we'll walk it down slowly, all the pain
and sorrow we've inherited, the guilt
of being human, of making bereft.

We'll tell our troubles to the air
in that birch grove beyond the ridge,
where the stone bridge is, where the river
flows smoothly into the heavy meadows,
before we walk quietly with the night's fall
home to our city sleeping by the sea.

Watercolour

I watch as you work the colour on soft paper,
watch as the wind and water come and go
eddying and gusting between mind and hand
as forms float in; your eye follows the brush.

Wash after wash, the shifting sway of thought.
Wash after wash, the sound of thought in silence

until something comes clear and you stand back,
surprised and not mistaken: now you've found it,
what you'd already guessed was already there.

So with our lives: the colours sift through wind
and water as we walk the Burrow Beach,
hung on the air for us, blessed and unsurprised

at what we find there always: that quiet weight
of breath and gesture, the shifting sway of thought,

the brushstroke of whatever makes our world.
My life has been all colour since that day
you wrote your address for me on soft paper,
the shape of our promised future already clear.

The Bodhisattvas That We Were
Are Still on the Road

Morning, sun in the trees, the road outside Killarney,
first harmonica and learning 'Love Minus Zero';
so earnest and clear, the long road before me,
ready for love and learning, ready to go.

Three bows to that very young man.

Three bows to the unquiet spirit of Jack Kerouac,
 to the lonely man in the dark nights where he sighs for the road,
wishes the road back again, would like to start over,
a great natural bedfellow lonesome in Carnac at the end

for morning, sun in the trees, the road outside himself,
the words tumbling in his head, love and zero balanced
clear, facing the highway and himself, hearing the long train
pull away into the far-off halls of night.

Three bows to that very young man.

Nel mezzo del cammin, or a little further on,
I stop what I'm doing to let the city roar past me,
to let myself fall all the way back to that morning
where the road began, and farther back —

Cork City Library, checking out *On The Road*,
staying up for a week of nights with the house asleep,
puzzling it all out, the wild hammering swoop of it,
the dizzy rising and falling and unfolding.

So many roads behind me now and the halls of night getting closer, the starry halls of night; I reach the book down from the shelves, knock a harmonica to the floor. I pick it up and blow: love minus zero, no limit.

Instructions

When the day comes, as it will, to lay me
down at last in the wet, black earth
choose what you will to remember,
let the rest spin away like leaves.

I am going nowhere.
I love this earth too much.
I could never love you enough but now
I have all the time there is to go on trying.

The Open Window

The yellow twist of the witch hazel
lifts its shy torch and the gorse at the gate
is budding and those slender things
that look like willows, bought
so long ago now in Donegal,
are still as the breeze falls;
pods of light and shade under the street lamp
in the rich, neat garden that you've made.

I let the floor fall away beneath me,
the walls dissolve and the desk & chair
and the books fly away until what is left is this:
me hovering above you in an empty cave
of light, you seated plain in the room below,
staring as I am at the world outside.
I float down and you float up and the mid-air
is where we come to rest.

Shoulder to shoulder and not a word said,
head inclined to head; your breath settles
and mine does and the metronome of fate
sounds in the echoing house — a strong beat
like a heartbeat, a certain sway in things,
a sense of time that's reticent and shy.
Here the year turns, as we turn now
and the gravid world turns in the halls of space.

What I'm most grateful for is grace —
I wanted to call down earlier and say so
but now instead, as your eyes open wide
and the house timbers settle in the heat, I let

my hands fly up to cup your head, my look
hold yours. Nothing that need be said.
A nod to winter, the miracle repeats —
look, all around us here in air
the new growth pushing through, strong and clear.

Cape Horn

I hand over the wheel and step aside,
I close my eyes, I think of you all, I open my arms
to this wind from the ice bound south,
sucked upward then bent towards long-imagined Africa
by the looming weight of the continent up above;

I feel the boat heel and dig deep as we drive on,
I want to say, as we crash through broken waters,
I will be gone as these under the keel are gone,
that we ride the wind a moment, a moment only,
but the better truth is this: time is eternal now,
there never was, nor ever will be, an end to voyaging.